THE ASH OF TIME

Penny Sharman

First published 2022 by The Hedgehog Poetry Press

Published in the UK by
The Hedgehog Poetry Press
5, Coppack House
Churchill Avenue
Clevedon
BS21 6QW

www.hedgehogpress.co.uk

ISBN: 978-1-913499-93-8

9 8 7 6 5 4 3 2 1

A CIP Catalogue record for this book is available from the British
Library.

Contents

The Clearing 5

Lessons from the larder floor 6

I am the girl 7

A room to sleep in 8

Architect of sleep 9

Purple 10

The girl with two hearts 11

Syzygy 12

Pandemic bedroom 13

Only the answer-birds 14

The resettlement of hearts 15

In the days of 16

Marauder's Map 18

The singing tree 19

Skin 20

Ode to my brain 21

A strange grief 22

Antistar 23

Vow Maker 24

The Ash of Time 25

I would like to dedicate The Ash of Time *to my three beautiful sons, Stephen, Mark and Gavin: it is only through being a parent to them that I have learnt so much about myself and how to love unconditionally.*

The Clearing

The slightest light
gathers through oak time—
leaves almost golden
and moss-moss—dark the green—
velvet under foot
crack the smallest of twigs
my breath in and out
skin with goose pimples
something cold in my lungs
and then you
eyes of stars
bright in this dawn
tales of you and me
you the barking deer
so brown and small
your time on earth
ancient
and me the bairn
in all of this
mulch and canopy

Lessons from the larder floor

I'm hiding in the larder—the cold small room with a sliding door—I'm small enough to sit under the stone slab where mum keeps the bread cheese and butter—I'm hiding from my brother who teases and goads me—chases me around the house—sometimes I run up the stairs over the red patterned Axminster carpet and I think the brass rungs are like jewels that shine and hold everything in place—sometimes I reach the bathroom and lock the door until he goes away—I sit on the loo and pray for a sister—it's taken me over fifty years to realise I don't get boys or men and I ask myself do I really like their different ways—I know I hate them in bovver boots—I know I like their kisses—I'm hiding in the larder—I can't reach the shelves which have jars full of mum's homemade strawberry jam and plum chutney— her pickled shallots—tin containers of flour and sugar—everything to feed our day to day hunger—through the crack in the door I see mum look at me—I read her mind—she tells me she's always been good and let men control her life—she whispers in my ear—run free girl—run wild—don't let men steal your zest—your dance for life—and I start to move my feet on the cold tiled floor—and I Isadora my way to freedom one year after another— sometimes I keep my mouth shut and give my spirit away— sometimes I bellow so loud I frighten the boys away and I never see them again—but I can laugh whenever I want—run upstairs—lie down on my big bed and just be me

I am the girl

who speaks in cabbages and mushrooms when each of you
leaves the arena of heart. Give me honey-glue to seal these lips.

In the local market cheese is my friend, chilli cheddar or anything
that crumbles between my mouth and yours.

Forgiveness like lemons, my smile upside down and God!
my knees are sore with penance—a whip would be quicker—

as if I have done something wrong—Heh!

Don't you like my loons, my fine tongue of truth?

I'm the old one now,
before I was a bird-girl flying higher than trees,

then you with a beard and silver hair
pulled me down by these claws.

I still watch the cave behind me as I leave stage right.
And even though I'm naked now, don't think I have forgotten.

By the way, the shopping basket full of oranges and cherries
has melted under the willow.

They say it's the hottest day ever and the river is dry.

A room to sleep in

Bedrooms are like lovers they come and go.

I lived with dolls and one brown teddy bear
in a small room with lemon walls where wind
wrapped herself around the side of the house like a whip.
I would wake before dawn and sneak into mum
and dad's bed to feel safe. I stopped going in after
I found dad lying on top of mum. I sucked my thumb for years.

My runaway rooms were filled with clocks ticking
as my skirts got shorter, my lips got plumper.
I longed for love and a double bed to share.
There was that one room where I lay in bed for days
with cramps and jellied blot clots fell to the wooden floor.
There was a marriage room where cruelty banged my head
against a bully boy, where my legs curled up so tight no one could find me.

Bedrooms are like lovers they come and go.

They are dreams on the hour hand that move without sound.
I found my room for one as time knocked loud on the door.
I made an art gallery of glass, canvas, textiles and fairies.
I hung them on my walls. I collected paperweights filled
with swirls of colour, my own cosmos filled with light.
I chose windows that looked on trees and hillsides, the vast
sky above crooked houses on New Earth Street.

Bedrooms are like lovers they come and go.

Architect of sleep

It's much darker now the tinsel and rainbow lights
are packed away and spiders dream of summer. But
it's never silent. Shadows exist on the wall behind
each picture. I swear they move when I'm asleep.
I stir with their creaks, I hear whispers about children—
the wars between us all.

I start again—listen to my heartbeat—slow it down—
slow in down—sip water.

If only I could hear the rhythm of tides lap
a shoreline—something regular to ground me
in this dark bed, something to numb the noise
of cars on tarmac, of trains and planes outside my door.

I used to hear the owl call to his lover across the valley.
I used to see them fly just before the dawn.

Purple

Today I picked up purple instead of watching water fall over Low Force.
I found one of the last harebells in the meadow, a tiny heather flower
high on the moorland and a wild scabious by the river.

Their purple whispers their grief in this open landscape, how all the
other blooms are gone now to soggy brown mulch, mould for the
underworld, lost to Hades.

But, these are the singular buds, still alive in the lea of the year,
in full sun that pours down from Holwick, they are blessed with
this one day where water is a storm force, where the copse, shaking

beech leaves preach a sermon of hard times to come, where I'm
sunbathing, trousers rolled up to my knees, arms bare to catch just
one hour of warmth on my flesh, on this day of purple in October gales.

The girl with two hearts

I guess it might be confusing,
twin organs that beat a day's story
out of sync with each other.

I wonder how they can
know the depth of each
tick-tock, drumbeat, all
that blood pumping
around the whole of her,
swish of hours, rumba
in the brain.

I'm curious about their
power to bridge emotion
with logic in a waterfall of
noise in a cavity under her
breastplate, if her rib-count
is still less than a man's?

I think she wrote a book
about timing. About vital
occasions where hearts
come together for comfort
then run out the door, or
when her two hearts held
yours far too tightly —
pit-of-a-blood-clot-black-blood.

She recently told me how
she had recognised a rhythm
in her other heart, a melody
so alike and how red
they both are,
how simple
their minutes
have become.

Syzygy

inside

    the glass weight
    an octopus
    blue bubble
    a still life
    tentacles
    a world within a world
    something hard

and there are three y's in this title

    why do I give you a hard time
    under a full moon
    secrets hold
    the answers
    to mood swings
    lack of blood-flow

    why is it constantly raining
    snow a memory
    and celandines
    flower before their time
    do they realise the danger

    why did today's dawn
    blaze so loud
    every shade of vermillion
    and orange
    a cocktail of
    everything pink
    when only minutes later
    sky is a grey uniform

inside

    the glass weight
    a blue monster
    phantom of an ocean
    that says something is
    connected in these words.

Pandemic bedroom

On the white windowsill I make an altar,
place my quartz, amethyst and rose crystals,
my eagle rattle to shake away fear, a hand made
embroidered card from Devon for creativity,
a replica of a Viking ship crewed by worry dolls,
a bleached driftwood stick that says

happiness comes in waves

In the dark night I hear scratching under white
floorboards and in the wattle and daub, it wakes
any peace I might have gathered under a duvet
in the green room. I think it's a portent, like rats
gnawing at my wooden box deep under the earth.

If I didn't have the window to gaze out at hope
I wouldn't see my treasures that hang from fences,
that lie under a twisted hazel,
my glitter ball of dancing days,
the angel with broken wings,
the Vettriano lovers kissing on the sand.

If I didn't have the window in the back bedroom
I might be starved of avian life, the shaking ritual
of the copper beech through another turn of our globe.
It's what keeps me sane, leaf thought falling to dirt,
miracles that wait under-land, the bluebells and
black geraniums asleep for now.

All of these remind me
I am no longer alone in this one room of heart.
And when I close my eyes to dream
it's always you,
my soft skinned wizard that holds me steady.

Only the answer-birds

Night

Look, here's my length, the indigo spine of me.
I bend down to the pain of your coming.

Look, here's my width, a lilac mother,
you an alien blue—something or someone,
my sugared almond heart
you a tiny green seaweed wriggle thing.

Look at the embryo breeze of you
hold on—hold on—hold on
to my powder puff love,

you inside of me—miracle blue-green
brushwork of stars.

Sunset

This is my only dance
black wisp of me
in a dust storm
the yellow cloud of lies
the minutes of me
white pretence
the cumulonimbus

you say I bully you
so where's my heart
in all this nebula talk
pow—punch—pow

look at my face
how I long to dive
into an ocean
of dark blue
bruise of me
mulch of green

The resettlement of hearts

Now that you've gone
it's just photographs or Skype time,

nothing concrete to hold onto,
nothing flesh and bone.

This golden chord attached to our hearts
has stretched too far. Even elastic has only one life.

Now that you've disappeared
a ghostly form of you exists in my mind.

I've lost the essence of you, juices
to the oceans and skies.

I've lost you to another universe
where you will live and I will die.

Now that you have flown
to unreachable towns, fields, mountains and seashores

how can I sew my heart back together?
How will I wake each day, shower, dress,

make breakfast and dinner, walk to the
other side of my valley?

In the days of

friendship   smiles   warm amber
golden beech leaves
dying

fragile our childish hearts
that play with life
on hopscotch squares
make words from sandpits
sing Crazy like Patsy Cline
remember joy
on the witch's hat

happy our flesh
hugs from the medicine box
close we came
to understanding
the perfect
combination
for scones cream and jam
our pinafores
full of acceptance
that
the use of butter
is always
an individual
choice

sad
the existence of
chaos
in our sumptuous meals
of companionship

the good wife
the moral sister
the harlot child

on days like these
where clag sticks firmly
over Saddleworth moor
weeping is all I have left
it drips drips drips
like blood from a cut

on days with blue and yellow
I dance barefoot
on wet grass
my eyes fixed
on the horizon

Marauder's Map

"I solemnly swear that I am up to no good"

One of the cruelest jokes—
eyes that watch your every move
as if they think they know
what you're really up to.

Even when a pretence of friendship
seems safe enough to sail to sea,
hoist the mainsail and take to
open water, let your hair down—
look how hearts pretend to stroke yours
with a mother's suckle. Awe, bless
the kindness of their understanding.

One of the harshest games—
maybe you know it,
a parlour compendium
for more than two players,
where the aim is to nitpick
a mate and bully, yes bully
a whole world into pieces.

Of course there will be red faces and tears.

"Mischief managed"

The singing tree

The rowan tree became an opera, a cacophony on the shoreline
where Morecambe mud forgets about her worry of water.

Now it's just a memory on her horizon of tides,
the rows between oystercatchers and herring gulls.

We came so close to sparrow-talk, symphony of dying leaves.

We heard an aria of love-notes, gossip of avian life.

We stood amazed by their loud-speak; every decibel touched our hearts,
our mouths holding a wish that we had the throttle to blare out such songs.

Skin

Each day I try to map myself, try to fathom
if I'm with my arms or legs, but each cell of me
morphs so bloody fast I can't compass my heart
or brain to pinpoint my existence.

When I'm asleep my skin, like wrapping paper,
loses a reason to be and remembers a mother's
soft cheek, a child's grazed knee, all monsters
that lie under my coat of skin.

When I look at the surface of my hand, I've become
my mother's atlas. I own her liver spots of art, her
freckles and love lines. I see how far my flesh has
stretched to contain the age of me.

Ode to my brain

I don't know how you do it all.
After all the years of planning, doing,
predicting the next steps,
crawling, standing, toddling, walking,
speaking, laughing, crying, learning by rote,
how to tie a shoelace,
yet still I don't know you at all.

You're amazing.
If all that's left of me is a mass of jelly,
oh how we would have felt the spectrum
of love and hate,
books, ideas, techniques,
such stuff, clutter, pain, joy.

I could hold you in
the palm of my hands,
a universe of contemplation,
a vastness of interstellar space,
wrinkled walnut spongy mushroom thing.

Oh how I love you,
you enchanted loom,
network of neurons.
Your obviously bigger on the inside.

A strange grief

Everything looks normal in the garden.
Bees still dine on nectar,
the robin, blackbird and jackdaw fixed
to timed habits of song and pecking.

But I'm lost.
I lead a chrysalis life.
I wait for the Albertine's buds to grow,
for a mock orange's perfume to flood the air.

I'm lost in clouds
above this small plot of dirt.
My hands long to touch my sons
far away from my strange grief,
solitude in the brain, something
that slips away like water falling over stones.

I wait for the buddleia
to flourish with purple flowers
and red admirals.
This strange grief
opens my eyes
to see yours in dreams,
see yours stare into mine.

Everything looks fine in the garden.
But my strange grief lingers,
a heavy metal in my heart;
and I am all to pieces
beside the dying columbine's
faithful flowers.

Antistar

Fluid me
skin & bone me
eyelash and freckle
old breasts——dry eyes

I let you all go to the dust of me

white hair——red lips——gravestone teeth
shiver of the child I knew

I let you all go to the dust of me

Soft mummy
Hard daddy

Fluid me
skin and bone me
song of an angel
song of a devil

I'm almost a drumbeat in your world
gone forever
my sibling chord
your smile
a peach memory
soft the hashish days
our common language
of joy

Vow Maker

after The Bride by Marc Chagall

When you`re in the dream everything is real,
the bride and groom riding a giant cockerel,
the girl with a blue fan covering her vagina.

There are many clouds in dreams   confusions in the brain,
the tiny man tucked within a bird`s wing,
the upside down angel with feathers of muslin.

Everyone`s flying of course, no one`s really on the ground.
The faraway village is made up of small houses and skyscrapers,
all the curtains are closed, we, the numbed faces stare, stare out.

When you`re in the dream everything is real,
leaves on the trees are green and clouds are everywhere,
ghosts in abundance.

The couples keep on coming through the doors,
wedded bliss like newly formed mountains...........

The Ash of Time

Every story mum told about her Indian home,
the monkeys in the garden,
her mum holding her tight,
a stranger's arms to replace them,
will go into the vault of un-forgetting.

Every musical we saw,
the song list of movies:

Bloody Mary, Bali Hai,
I'm goin to wash that man right out of my hair:

all those technicolour days
will fade into the cavern of un-forgetting.

But there will always be
something left in the ash of time—

her high cheek bones
her freckled hands
and the way she asked me
at the end

what's it all about
this life
this life